River Stone Baby Birds

Paint a Colorful Aviary on Rocks

Tuzi Williams

For everyone who loves cool rocks.

About the author

Tuzi Williams lives in Radium Springs, New Mexico, by the Rio Grande river. Her animal-themed artwork, custom tile and crafts are enjoyed worldwide. Tuzi's other books include "Who's in the Moon?", "Creating Your Own Yucca Pets" and "Captain Jack Rabbit."
You can email Tuzi at tqwilliams52@gmail.com.

Copyright © 2012 Tuzi Williams
All rights reserved. No portion of this book may be reproduced in any form without permission in writing by the author.

ISBN-13: 978-1469900230

Cover Designed by
Michael Sandoval

Digital formatting by
T.V. Williams / Reality Bytes
Las Cruces, NM

TABLE OF CONTENTS

INTRODUCTION	4
TOOLS AND PAINTS	5
PREPARATION	7
BABY BIRD BASICS	8
BABY ROBIN	12
BABY CARDINAL	17
BABY GOLDFINCH	22
BABY BLUE JAY	27
BABY CHICK	32
BABY DUCKLING	36
BABY HUMMINGBIRD	41
BABY QUAIL	48
BABY WOODPECKER	53
BABY PARROT	58
BABY TERN	63
BABY "RED, WHITE and BLUE BIRD"	67
BABY CROW	72
"MY LITTLE CHICKADEE"	76
OWLET	80
"BEGGING BABIES"	85
"EARLY BIRDS"	86

INTRODUCTION

Painting on stones has been a favorite art form for years - but what can be done with all of those wonderful, palm-sized, smoothed and rounded river stones?

Over a decade ago I came up with a way to paint appealing baby birds on river stones. Since then, I've created thousands of them, to sell at wildlife art shows, our famous Las Cruces Farmers and Crafts Market, and, of course, to give as "tweet" little gifts. Small birds are special, unexpected accents around your home. Larger ones can be fun paperweights.

Painting on small river stones is rewarding . You use very little paint and even a few tiny strokes of paint can yield a great deal of detail. A small size generally means they're faster to paint than a large stone. If you sell the birds, a smaller price may be necessary, but they are so charming that you will always have customers! They make great purse or pocket pets, and I even have a customer who always carries a few with her, to drop off as unexpected anonymous "gifts" for waitresses and medical office staff. The baby birds pack a big punch in a small package - they make people smile.

Now I'd like to share my baby birds, and I hope you enjoy them as much as I do. With just a stone, a little paint and patience, you can create a "cheep" but appreciated gift for any occasion.

TOOLS AND PAINTS

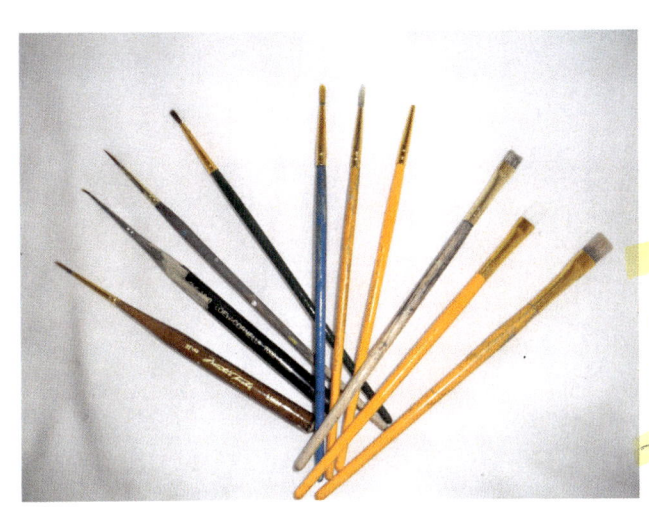

Brushes are your sole tools. Have on hand an assortment of brushes including a fine 18/0 or 20/0 liner or detail brush, a #0 round for general brushwork, flat, soft-bristled brushes for broad coverage and a stiff-bristled brush for dry-brushed areas. Try to get the best brushes you can afford - they'll serve you well for many years if you care for them. As you continue to paint, your basic brush collection will grow and you'll be able to select the perfect brush for any need.

I use acrylic paints in the 2 ounce plastic bottles. They're inexpensive, easy to find, and easy to clean up. A good selection will include black, white, red, dark brown, medium brown, tan, orange, pink, terra cotta, light yellow, bright yellow, ochre, gray, royal blue, light blue, sage green, dark green, leaf green and yellow-green. These paints can be easily

blended to create even more colors. Various brands are available with slightly different color names and tones. Don't be afraid to substitute a

,htly different color than my projects call for! Acrylic paints are fast-ying and can be painted over, in case you make a mistake or want to change something.

Purchase a good-quality varnish or sealer to apply over your finished project. Varnish will brighten your colors and protect your paints. Whether you choose a matte, satin or gloss varnish, or a spray-on or brush-on varnish, be sure it is non-yellowing. My favorite varnish is a brush-on acrylic satin varnish by Liquitex.

I recommend that you keep your birds indoors or in a protected area outside. However, I have had some outdoors in our desert sun, wind and monsoons for ten years now, and they still look good - there has been some fading, but otherwise the paint is fine.

Before you begin, gather some paper towels, old plastic dish lids for paint palettes, an old plastic bowl for brush rinsing, and wax paper to put under your birds when you varnish them.

PREPARATION

If you live by a sea coast, river or lake, you'll probably have no trouble finding great bird stones. I can usually find stones during walks; roadsides are sometimes a good source. Landscaping shops often carry rounded stones to put around potted plants. Department stores sometimes stock small bags or jars of these stones in their craft or floral sections. Never take stones from landscaped yards or businesses. Also, some beaches and parks prohibit the removal of any materials, including stones.

The best stones are palm sized but you can use larger ones or even tiny ones. Smooth, rounded or oval stones are the easiest to work with. The most important aspect of your bird will be its head, so try to imagine a rounded head area on your stone which will accommodate the head and beak. Owlet stones usually "sit up" on a flat base. As you can see from the photo, even stones that are quite irregular or flattened can be used.

Whether you gather one stone or many, be sure to rinse them to remove dirt or debris. Let them dry, and you're ready to paint.

 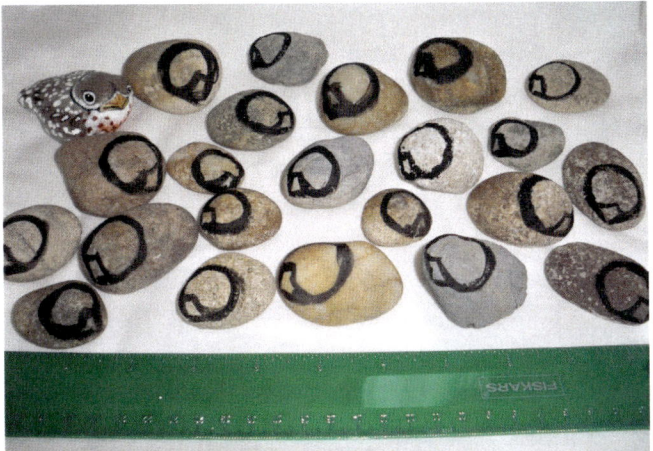

BABY BIRD BASICS

In real life, baby birds seldom resemble adult birds. They're mostly drab and gray to camouflage them in their defenseless stage. I've taken the liberty of giving my baby birds a big dash of adult coloration. The resulting babies are whimsical yet recognizable, with charming baby bird features.

It's almost impossible to get a realistic look by fully painting both of the bird's eyes. I've developed a type of perspective for my birds' heads. One eye will be cocked upward, and the other eye is only partially shown. By painting the bird's head this way, it will appear that the bird is tilting his head up to look at you - even on a very flat stone.
Additionally, the beak is drawn in a non-symmetrical manner. One side will be shown longer than the other.

 Here is the basic head, beak and eye layout for most of my birds:

Looking down at the top of the stone, the head is drawn round, unless the bird has a crest, and is about 1/2 the length of the stone. The beak is about 1/2 the width of the head.

Decide the best head placement for your stone. The head and beak should both fit on the top surface, close to the edge. A beak that slopes over the edge will never look right. Make sure that you'll be able to draw the tail at the opposite end.

Basic tail layout, looking at the bird from the tail end - paint the feathers like a fan. They should meet under the bird's rump.

Painting a basic beak, step-by-step: Use a detail brush. Some babies will have a different beak but this one is the most common. The mouth line and yellow detailing is painted in the same manner although the beak shape may be different. The project instructions will help you visualize this.

① Paint beak terra cotta

② Outline beak with Black
③ Black mouth line

④ Detail beak with light yellow

Eye detail

Most of the baby birds have big black eyes. Eyeliner is added to define them. This is usually white with an additional darker liner around it. A "gleam" (white dot) is then added at the same spot of each eye, to animate your baby bird.

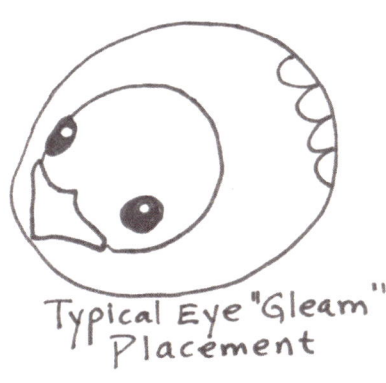

Typical Eye "Gleam" Placement

Feet and bottom of bird

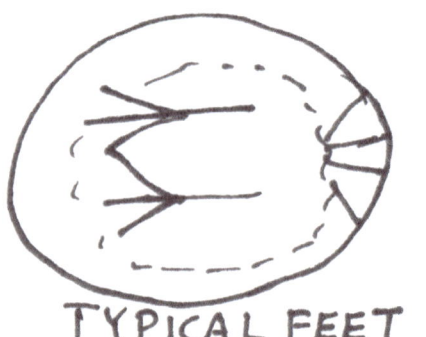

People do notice the bottom of your birds and are delighted to find feet! I generally bring my birds' body paint slightly onto the bottom of the stone, but leave the center unpainted. This is to let the natural stone show, to give Mother Nature her due. I paint the feet and add my initials in this bare area. Be sure your bird's feet are appropriate for its species and point towards the head of the bird, not the tail. Always initial or sign your baby bird. It is a work of art!

"Feather Dots"

Most of my project instructions call for "feather dots". These are a series of "U" shaped dotted markings on the birds' backs, done with a small pointed brush. The dots suggest fluffy, mottled baby feathers. I paint them row by row like fish scales until the desired area is filled.

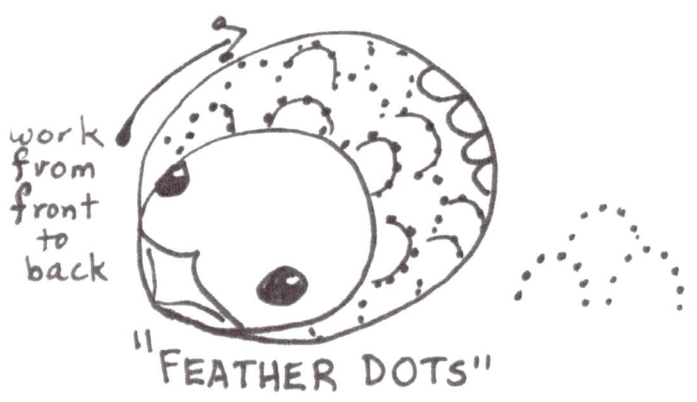

Avoid the head and tail area and any wing feathers. Begin your "feather dots" behind the bird's head and work backwards toward the tail area, using a scaled pattern.

"Dry Brush" technique

Some of the instructions call for you to use a "dry brush" technique. This technique will give you a soft coloration over other colors and will give a downy look. To dry brush, dip a fairly stiff brush into your paint. Wipe off almost all the paint onto a paper towel. "Scrub" the brush onto the desired area until you get the color intensity you want.

"Wash" technique

Add water to your paint to get a very dilute, watery color. Use a soft brush to gently "wash" this color over the desired area. The color underneath should still show through; if not, your "wash" is not dilute enough. If the wash paint runs, gently wipe off the drips with a paper towel.

Additional notes

In my instructions, "beak" and "bill" are interchangeable.
The initial black outline around the head is important; it will provide a dark area to highlight the feather strokes around the head. You don't want it to be too wide and obvious, but if you accidentally paint over it, be sure to draw it in again.

BABY ROBIN

Paints you'll need:
taupe or gray; black; white; terra cotta; medium brown; brick red; light yellow; bright yellow

1. Outline head and beak with black paint.

2. Paint head and back taupe.

3. Paint chest white.

4. Dry brush a small area of brick red across the lower chest.

5. Paint the beak terra cotta.

6. With a detail brush, paint the eyes black. Add black mouth lines. Paint the tail outlines in black.

7. Paint the beak details with light yellow.

8. Dry brush brown across the top of the head and on the body, avoiding the tail.

9. With a detail brush, outline the eyes with white. Add tiny white feather strokes around the head extending into the black outline. Add a white line just above the beak.

10. Add a little black to the gray to get a darker gray. Outline around the white eyeliner and also over the white line above the beak.

11. Paint two or three bands of white across all of the tail feathers.

12. Paint white feather dots on the robin's body, on the taupe areas only.

13. With your detail brush, paint two or three parallel rows of brown dots from the beak to the bottom of the chest as shown.

14. Give each eye a "gleam".

15. On the stone's bottom, paint the feet with bright yellow and add your initials.

16. Varnish your baby robin using wax paper underneath.

BABY CARDINAL

aints you'll need:
black; white; red; brick red; orange; terra cotta; light yellow

1. Outline head and beak with black paint.

2. Paint head and chest red. You may need two coats.

3. Paint the rest of the back, including the tail area, with brick red.

4. Paint the beak terra cotta.

5. With a detail brush and black paint, paint the eyes, mouth line, tail feather outlines and the black "bib" directly under the beak. Paint a thin black line directly above the beak.

6. Outline the eyes with white.

7. Add light yellow beak details.

8. Outline the eyes again, this time with black. Connect the black eye outline to the black line over the beak.

9. Switch to orange paint. With the detail brush, outline the beak above the black line. Outline the black eye "mask" and paint tiny strokes around the head. Stroke in orange bands across the tail feathers.

10. With red paint, add a red tip to the top of each tail feather.

11. Excluding the head, chest and tail, paint orange "feather dots."

12. Add a white "gleam" in each eye.

13. Paint feet using light yellow and add your initials.

14. Varnish your baby cardinal, with wax paper underneath.

BABY GOLDFINCH

Paints you'll need:
black, white, terra cotta, light yellow, bright yellow, orange, gray

1. Outline the head and beak with black.

2. With bright yellow, paint the head, chest and a triangle on the back behind the head. You may need two coats.

3. Paint the wings, tail area, and the back, except for the yellow triangle, black.

4. Paint the beak terra cotta.

23

5. With a stiff brush, dry-brush the top of the head black. Leave a yellow border around the black area. You can dry-brush right up to the beak, however.

6. With a detail brush, paint black eyes, the mouth line and a black line over the beak.

7. Paint the beak detail light yellow.

8. Add tiny light yellow strokes around the head.

9. Outline the eyes with white and then with black.

10. Sketch in the tail outline with gray paint.

11. With your round brush, add a few white wing feather strokes as shown. Add white accents to the tail as shown.

12. Add water to a drop of orange paint to get a very dilute orange. Use a soft, flat brush to quickly stroke orange across the top of the chest and on the yellow triangle behind the head. Don't completely cover these areas with orange wash, however - most of the areas should remain bright yellow.

13. Paint a white "gleam" in each eye.

14. Paint the goldfinch's feet with light yellow and initial your stone.

15. Varnish your baby goldfinch using wax paper underneath.

BABY BLUE JAY

Paints you'll need:
black, white, terra cotta, light yellow, royal blue, light blue

1. Paint the head and beak with black.

2. Following pictures, sketch in the wing line and head markings with pencil.

3. Paint royal blue on the wings, back and tail area and across the top of the head.

4. Paint the chest and cheek areas white.

5. Paint the beak terra cotta.

6. With a detail brush, paint the eyes, mouth line and tail outline with black paint.

7. Add beak details with light yellow paint.

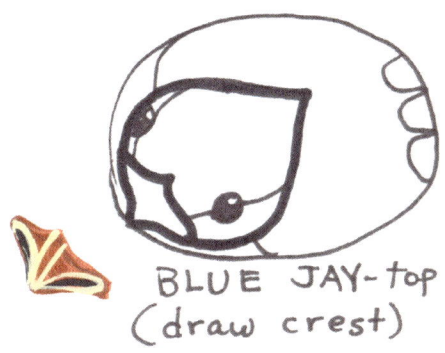 

8. With a stiff brush, dry-brush light blue on the top of the head and on the blue "shoulder" areas.

9. Use your detail brush and light blue to stroke tiny feather lines around the head.

29

10. Dry-brush a black "V" across the white chest, as shown.

11. Stroke in bands of white across the tail feathers.

12. With a detail brush, outline the eyes with white then outline again in royal blue. Paint a thin white line above the beak. Add a few white strokes along the bottom of the cheeks.

13. With a round brush, paint several strokes of white along the wing area to suggest wing bars.

14. Add "feather dots" everywhere except on the head and tail.

15. Paint a white "gleam" in each eye.

16. Give your bird feet using light yellow and initial your piece.

17. Varnish your baby blue jay using wax paper underneath.

BABY CHICK

Baby chicks are so fluffy and have a wide breast, so set the head and beak back a little.

Paints you'll need:
black, white, terra cotta, light yellow, bright yellow, orange, ochre, gray

1. Outline the head and beak with black.

2. Paint the head and body bright yellow. You'll probably need two coats.

3. With a detail brush, paint the beak terra cotta and add a black mouth line.

4. With gray paint, draw just three or four stubby little tail feathers.

CHICK - side
(shows wing)

5. Switch to pale yellow paint and a stiff-bristled brush. Dry brush light yellow on the cheek, top of head, wing area, the breast under the beak and the tail feathers. Use a detail brush to paint tiny light yellow strokes around the head to suggest downy feathers. Finally, paint the beak details in light yellow.

CHICK - top
(pointed bill)

6. Thin a little ochre paint to get a dilute paint. With your round brush, apply strokes of paint just behind the head and under the dry-brushed wing and chest area. This will make your lighter features appear to "pop."

7. Paint the eyes black. Outline them with white.

8. With the round brush, add several short strokes of white on the wings to suggest new feathers.

9. With a detail brush and ochre paint, outline the eyes again and paint a shadow in front of each eye as well as a short line behind each eye, as shown. Paint an ochre line just above the beak. Flick a few tiny ochre lines above each eye to suggest eyebrows.

10. With white paint, add a few feather strokes under the eyes to highlight the chick's puffy cheeks. Add a "gleam" to each eye.

11. Paint the feet with orange paint and add your initials.

12. Varnish your baby chick, using wax paper underneath.

BABY DUCKLING

Ducklings have large, rounded bills, so set the head further back from the stone's edge to allow the bill to show. This duckling is a classic white Pekin duckling, but other duck varieties have ducklings with interesting colors and markings.

Paints you'll need:
black; white; brown; bright yellow; light yellow; orange; gray; pink, terra cotta

1. Outline the head and bill with black. Also draw the wing and tail outlines with black.

DUCKLING -side (shows wing)

2. Paint the head and body light yellow, avoiding the black outlines.

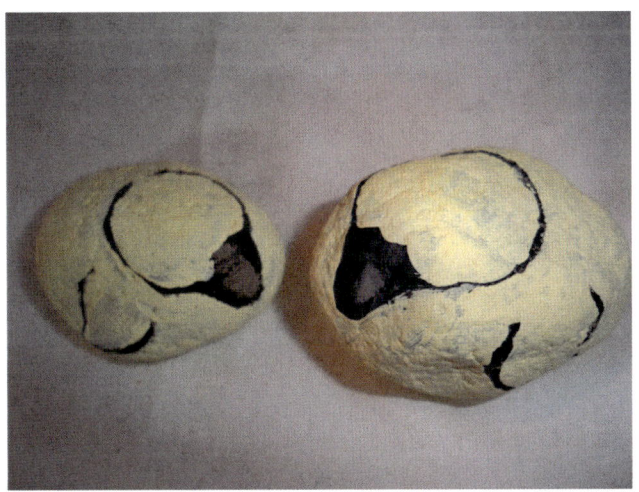

3. Mix a little pink with the light yellow to get a flesh color. Paint the bill with this.

4. With a flat, stiff brush, dry-brush bright yellow on the top of the head, across the tops of the wings and on the back behind the head..

5. Dry-brush white on the chest and belly, as far as the tail.

6. With your round brush, add a few short white wing feather strokes and fill in the tail feathers with white.

7. Mix some orange into the bright yellow. Dilute this with water to make a wash. Add this wash behind the head and over the "shoulders."

8. With ochre paint, paint an oval over the areas where the eyes will go and add ochre lines between each tail and wing feather to "separate" them.

9. Paint the eyes black, then outline them with white. Outline each eye again with brown.

10. With a detail brush and white paint, paint tiny lines around the head and wings to suggest tiny feathers. Add a few white lines to the back of the duckling as shown.

11. Detail the beak as shown, using white and terra cotta.

12. Paint a white "gleam" in each eye.

DUCKLING - top
(longer, rounded bill)

13. Paint the feet as shown in orange and outline them with brown. If possible, paint the feet near the front of the duckling's chest, and show them peeking out! Initial your stone.

14. Varnish your baby duckling using wax paper underneath.

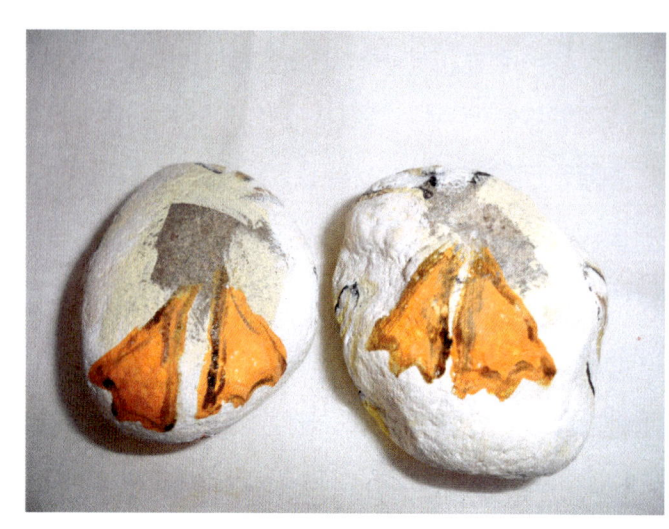

BABY HUMMINGBIRD

If you feel confident painting in miniature, the tiniest round stone can become a cute baby hummer.

Paints you'll need:
black; white; red; terra cotta; sage green; dark green; yellow-green; gray; light yellow; ochre

1. Outline the head and beak with black. With black, draw the outlines of the wings and also draw in the eyes and outline the white cheek area beneath them.

2. Paint the head, back and wing area with sage green.

42

3. Paint the cheeks and chest area white.

4. Fill in the wing area with black, extending to the very back of the bird. The wings should meet at the very back bottom.

5. Paint six small white dots just underneath where the wings meet in the back - these will be the tail feather tips.

6. With a flat, stiff brush and dark green, dry-brush over the sage green area of the head, directly behind the head, the shoulders, and the "V" area above the tail.

7. With a detail brush, add a few bright green dots to the top of the head, and paint bright green "feather dots" on the shoulders and back. Add a few random dots of light yellow to these areas also.

8. Water down a drop of terra cotta paint to get a thin wash. Carefully wash a little of this on each shoulder, down the middle of the back and on top of the head.

9. Paint the beak gray. Add light yellow lines to define it. There is no mouth line on this bird.

HUMMING BIRD – top
(short, pointed bill)

10. Paint the eyes black, outline them with white, and then add another outline with black.

11. With the round brush and gray paint, stroke 3 wing feather lines down both black wing areas.

12. Using the detail brush and black paint, paint a series of parallel dashes on the white cheeks and chest as shown. Add a dot of red at the bottom of each line of dashes. When this has dried, make a thin wash from the red paint. Carefully add a "blush" of this wash to the chest area just underneath the beak.

13. With the detail brush, paint tiny white lines around the head and at the wing/shoulder junctures to highlight these areas.

14. Add a white "gleam" to each eye.

15. Paint the feet with ochre paint and initial your bird.

16. Varnish your baby hummingbird using wax paper underneath.

BABY QUAIL

Try using stones that "sit up" a little.

Paints you'll need:
black; white; brown; light yellow; tan; bright yellow; gray; terra cotta

1. Outline the head and beak with black. Also with black, outline the wing area, back stripes and the tail feathers.

QUAIL - side view

2. Paint the head, chest and back (between the stripes) with tan.

3. Paint the wings brown.

49

4. Paint the beak gray.

5. With a detail brush, paint the eyes black and add a black mouth line.

6. Also with black, outline the middle, arrow-shaped marking on top of the head. Fill this area with terra cotta paint.

7. With white and your round brush, paint two rows of dots across each wing.

8. Outline all of your wing edges with black paint and sharpen the back stripes if necessary. Paint several black dots underneath the white wing dots.

9. With the detail brush, stroke several bands of brown paint across the tail feathers.

10. Paint some tiny white dots on the chest directly in front of the wings.

11. Outline the eyes with white, and then add an additional black outline.

12. Paint a somewhat ragged black band extending from the back of each eye to the back of the head, curving to meet the tip of the "arrowhead" shape.

13. With the detail brush and light yellow paint, add the beak details. Add a stroke of light yellow above each black eye outline. Stroke a series of tiny lines around the head, on the chest, and down the tan back stripes. Switch to brown paint and add 4 or 5 tiny lines above the beak.

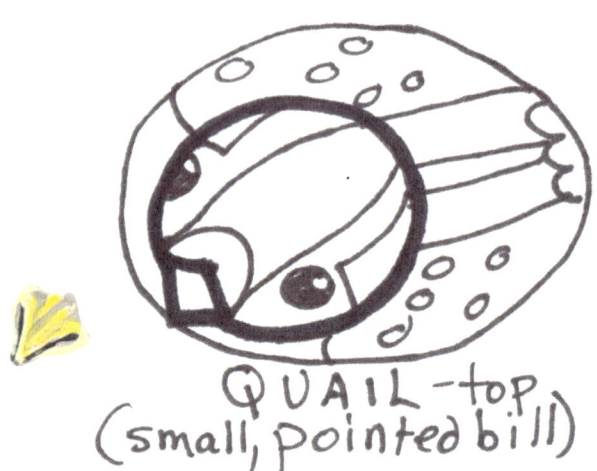

14. With the flat, stiff brush, dry-brush a little white over the terra cotta head stripe.

15. Add a white "gleam" to each eye.

16. Paint the feet with bright yellow. Add some water to the bright yellow to get a wash. Wash this very lightly across the beak.

Initial your stone.

17. Varnish your baby quail using wax paper underneath.

BABY WOODPECKER

There are many species of woodpeckers but I've chosen the (probably extinct) ivory-billed woodpecker for this project because of its unique coloration and patterns.

Paints you'll need:
black; white; red; gray; light yellow; bright yellow; orange

1. Outline the head and beak with black.

2. Using the diagrams and black paint, outline the body markings and eyes.

WOODPECKER-top (large, pointed bill)

WOODPECKER (side view)

3. Fill in the black areas as indicated.

4. Fill in the white areas as indicated.

5. Paint the bill gray.

6. Paint the crest area red as shown. You may need two coats.

7. With your flat, stiff brush and gray paint, dry-brush highlights over all of the black areas. Then, dry-brush a little gray over each of your white areas. Don't overdo it! A suggestion of contrast is all it takes.

8. Where the black areas meet, delineate them with tiny white feather strokes.

9. With the detail brush, paint tiny orange lines outlining the red crest. Paint a few orange strokes within the crest area also.

10. Add 2 or 3 gray lines on the white wing area to suggest wing feathers. Also with gray, outline several stubby tail feathers. Fill them with a few strokes of the gray.

11. Paint the eyes bright yellow. Add round black pupils in the centers. Be sure the eyes remain outlined in black. Paint the black mouth line.

12. Mix light yellow with white to get an even paler yellow. Use this to paint the beak details.

13. With light yellow, add a few tiny lines at the edges of the red crest.

14. Use the detail brush and gray paint to paint "feather dots" on the black areas of the body except the head and chest.

15. Paint a white "gleam" in each eye.

16. Woodpeckers have "zygodactyl" feet, meaning two toes point forwards and two point backwards. It's easy to paint their feet - an "X" will work! Paint the feet with bright yellow and initial your stone.

17. Varnish your baby woodpecker using wax paper underneath.

BABY PARROT

Paints you'll need:
black; white; red; bright yellow; light yellow; ochre; leaf green; sage green; dark green; yellow-green

1. Outline the head and beak with black.

2. Paint the head and body leaf green.

3. Paint the chest sage green.

4. With a stiff brush, dry-brush sage green on top of the head and over the body.

5. Draw the tail feathers with black paint.

6. Paint a red forehead above the beak, extending between the eyes. Paint two red wing bars on each wing.

7. Paint bright yellow wing bars above each of the red bars. Paint the tops of the tail feathers with bright yellow.

8. Fill in the beak area with ochre.

9. Paint the eyes black. When this dries, paint a circular iris with ochre. You can leave a central black "pupil" or add it later over the dry ochre paint.

10. With a detail brush, add a white outline around each eye.

11. Paint the mouth line black and outline the entire beak with a thin black line.

12. Detail the beak with light yellow. Add a black nostril dot on each side of the beak's midsection. With orange paint, stroke a few lines above the beak onto the red forehead. Brighten the beak sections with a hint of orange, also.

13. Still using the detail brush, switch to yellow-green paint. Add another line around the white eye line with the yellow-green. Paint tiny strokes around the head. Add yellow-green "feather dots" to the body, avoiding the chest and the wing bars. Add a few yellow-green band across the tail feathers.

14. Be sure your parrot has its black eye pupils, then add a white "gleam" to each eye.

15. Like woodpeckers, parrots are also zygodactyl. Paint an "X" for each foot, using light yellow. Initial your stone.

16. Varnish your baby parrot, using wax paper underneath.

BABY TERN

Leave no stone un-terned!" The common tern can be found near coastlines.

Paints you'll need:
black; white; gray; red; orange; brown; ochre

1. Outline the head and beak with black.

2. With pencil, draw the line between white and black markings on the face, using the diagram as a guide. Paint the top of the head black, and the bottom part white.

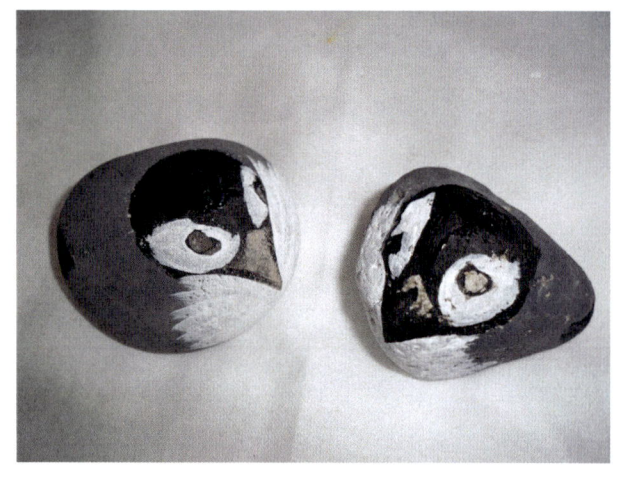

3. With black paint, sketch an "M" shape on the tail end to suggest a forked tail.

4. Paint the back gray. Fill in the chest area with white. Paint the tail feathers black.

5. Mix brown paint with water to get a dilute paint. Wash this thin brown paint lightly over the back behind the head and on the wing area.

6. Outline both of the tail feathers with a thin white line.

7. Paint the beak red. You may need two coats.

8. Paint the eye black. Outline it in white, then add an additional outline with black.

9. Using your detail brush, stroke tiny white lines all around the head.

10. Paint a black mouth line. Detail the mouth with ochre.

11. Paint white "feather dots" on the gray area of your bird.

TERN - top (pointed bill)

12. Paint the pointed tip of the beak black.

13. Give both eyes a white "gleam".

14. Refer to the photo to see how your tern's feet should look. Paint them in red, close to the front of the bird, as if they're tucked under its chest. Initial your stone.

15. Varnish your baby tern, using wax paper underneath.

"One good tern deserves another!" Here are twin terns, painted on an elongated stone. You can paint any of my bird designs as twins. Be sure to paint them the same size on the stone and separate them by a dark shadowed area. Heart-shaped stones work very well for "twins".

BABY "RED, WHITE and BLUE BIRD"

These would be great decorations or favors for patriotic holidays, but you could enjoy them anytime.

Paints you'll need:
black; white; red; royal blue; terra cotta; light yellow; light blue; gray; ochre

1. Outline the head and beak with black.

2. Paint the entire bird, except for the beak and chest area, with royal blue.

3. Paint the chest red. You may need two coats.

4. With pencil, draw the eyes and mark the head's cheek area.

5. Paint the eyes black and the cheek area white.

6. Outline the tail feathers with black.

7. Mix the red with a little white to get pink. Dry-brush a "blush" of this color on the red chest.

8. With a stiff, flat brush, dry-brush a little light blue on the top of the head, the back and the sides.

9. With your round brush, stroke white edges on the tail feathers. Add a few strokes on the sides of the bird to suggest short wing feathers. Paint white "feather dots" on the back.

10. Using the detail brush, stroke tiny white lines around the head. Outline the eyes with white then add another outline with gray. Paint a thin gray line above the beak.

11. Paint the beak with terra cotta. Add a black mouth line then detail the beak with light yellow.

12. Paint a white "gleam" in each eye.

13. Paint the feet with ochre paint and initial your stone.

14. Varnish your baby "red, white and blue bird" using wax paper underneath.

BABY CROW

Paints you'll need:
black; white; gray; red; ochre; bright yellow

1. Paint the entire stone black and let it dry.

2. With a pencil, outline the head, beak and tail. Also mark your eye placement.

3. Paint the eyes with bright yellow. Add a black pupil.

4. With a detail brush and gray paint, stroke tiny gray lines around the head to suggest bristly baby feathers. Also with gray, add a series of wing strokes, a couple of quick lines in the tail feathers, and "feather dots" on the crow's back. Arch a gray semicircle over each eye and paint a thin gray line above the beak. Add a few very small random dots on the top of the head.

5. Paint the beak red. You may need two coats. Let dry, then add a black mouth line, and detail the beak with ochre paint.

6. With the detail brush, add a couple of small white strokes over the upper part of the ochre beak detailing as shown. This will highlight the beak.

7. Give both eyes a white "gleam".

8. Paint the feet with bright yellow and initial your stone.

9. Varnish your baby crow using wax paper underneath.

"MY LITTLE CHICKADEE"

A small round stone can work well for this tiny bird.

Paints you'll need:
black; white; dark gray; light gray; light yellow; bright yellow

1. Outline the head and beak with black.

2. Outline the wings, back area, tail feathers and facial features with black.

3. Paint the wings dark gray. Paint the back and tail light gray. Paint the chest white.

4. Paint the cheek area white. Switch to black and paint the top of the head black. Also, add a black triangular-shaped area on the white chest directly under the beak.

5. Stroke a few lines of dark gray onto the tail feathers and fill in the beak with dark gray. With the detail brush, paint a thin dark gray line above the beak and add several tiny strokes along the back of the head on the black area.

6. Paint the eyes black. Outline them with white then outline the lower white eye line with dark gray. Add tiny white strokes around the head.

7. Paint a few quick, short strokes of white on each wing to suggest feathers. Paint white "feather dots" on the light gray area of the back.

8. With the detail brush, paint the black mouth line. Add beak details with light yellow.

9. Paint a white "gleam" in each eye.

10. Paint the feet with bright yellow and initial your stone.

11. Varnish "Your Little Chickadee" using wax paper underneath.

OWLET

Great horned owlets are basically fluffy balls with eyes and a beak. They don't have their ear tufts yet but do have distinctive facial features. They're cute and fun to paint; the only detailing you'll really have to do is the eyes. Choose rounded river stones with a flat bottom that will sit up and "look" at you.

Paints you'll need:
black; white; dark gray; terra cotta; bright yellow; ochre

1. Paint your entire stone dark gray and let it dry.

2. With a pencil, draw the eyes and beak. The eyes should be about 1 eye-width apart. Make sure the eyes are the same size and in proportion to your stone. The beak extends to about halfway up between the eyes.

3. Also with pencil, draw a semi-circular shape around the outside edge of each eye as shown.

4. With your detail brush, paint over all of your pencil lines with black paint.

5. With the round brush and black paint stroke six lines on the back of the owl for "wings". The bottom lines should actually go down to the bottom of the stone. Let dry.

6. Now comes the fun part - with a stiff-bristled brush and white paint, quickly stipple little "puffs" of downy feathers all over your owl, avoiding the wing lines and facial features. It's OK if you get a little paint on these features, however. Try to be random and let the gray background show through. Let dry.

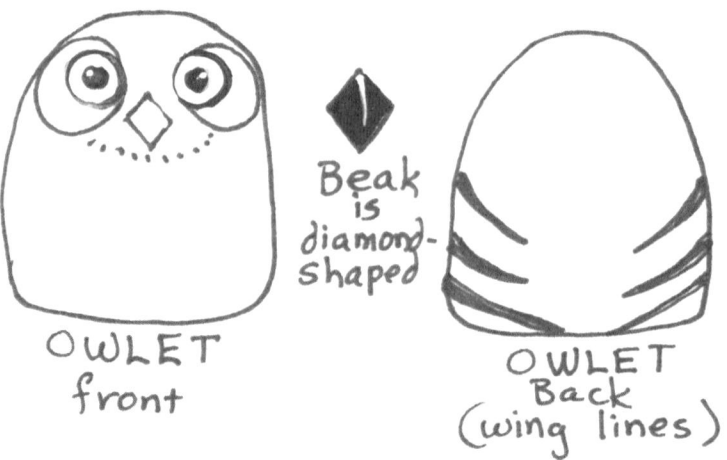

7. Add water to a drop of ochre paint to make a very dilute paint. Use a wide, soft brush to "wash" a little of this on the chest, head and back areas. Don't overdo - the bird should still be mostly white.

8. Paint the beak black. Paint the semicircles around the eyes terra cotta. Carefully fill in the eyes with bright yellow. You may need two coats of the yellow, and you may also need to redefine the eye circles with black.

9. With the round or detail brush, paint a black line around the outer edge of the eyes' semicircles, and add a black semicircle slightly below the beak, connecting to the terra cotta semicircles. Go over the black around the eyes again, to give this area depth.

10. Paint a thin white line down the middle of the beak to highlight it. Add longer white strokes above the beak extending into the forehead area; around each eye and beside the beak for a white "mustache"; and add smaller white strokes beneath the beak above the black semicircle.

11. Paint a round black pupil in the center of each eye.

12. Give both eyes white "gleams". Also, a few tiny white dots on the outer edges of the terra cotta semicircles will brighten your owl's face.

13. Owls, like woodpeckers and parrots, have zygodactyl feet. Paint them as large "X"'s with ochre paint. Initial your stone.

14. Varnish your owlet, using wax paper underneath.

"BEGGING BABIES"

The key to creating these babies is to set the head far enough back to draw the wide-open mouth. Draw your bird as usual but change the normal beak to a wide-open one. Refer to photos of baby birds to get insights into how these actually look. The further eye may be hidden by the beak.

The beak is first painted ochre. Paint the throat black, then add a pink tongue. Make a watery wash with terra cotta and carefully wash the interior of the beak, avoiding the outer edges, throat and tongue. Finally, outline the beak with light yellow to highlight the edges. Be sure the black outline around the beak remains crisp.

"EARLY BIRDS"

"The early birds get the worms."
Paint any bird from start to finish as instructed. Then, paint a wiggly-looking curvy pink line coming out both sides of the beak. With your detail brush, outline the pink worm with a thin black line. Switch to dark brown and paint small, parallel "segment" lines down the length of the worm's body. Add a tiny white dash across the top of each segment to suggest a "slimy" reflection. Yum! Baby bird breakfast is served.

Made in the USA
Coppell, TX
20 March 2021